PRAGUE
THE CITY AT A GLANCE

C000067235

Prague Castle
The city's pre-eminent landmark
affair of churches, palaces and p
offices. Proper exploration coul
Hradčanské náměstí, T 224 372 4

Trója Château
Elegant gardens front French architect Jean
Baptiste Mathey's baroque villa, which hosts
a collection of 19th-century Czech art. It
closes to the public from November to April.
U trojského zámku 1, T 283 851 614

St Nicholas Church
Kilián Ignác Dientzenhofer's 1735 church
boasts a dazzling baroque interior.
Malostranské náměstí

Josefov
Bar several synagogues and an extremely
overcrowded cemetery, little is left of the
city's former Jewish ghetto, now one of
Prague's most upmarket shopping areas.

Karlúv most (Charles Bridge)
Saintly statues line the cobblestoned crossing
linking Malá Strana and Staré Město.

National Memorial
Extensive renovations have diminished the
lingering communist associations but not
the powerful presence of this vast granite
complex topping Vítkov Hill.
See p010

Tower Park
Built during the Soviet occupation, this
rocket-like tower is rumoured to have been
erected to jam Western broadcasts. Climbing
up the outside is Czech artist David Černý's
surreal 2000 installation *Babies*.
See p068

INTRODUCTION
THE CHANGING FACE OF THE URBAN SCENE

It's hard to imagine now, but before the Velvet Revolution, Prague was a grey, rather mournful place to be – monumentally medieval, with cobbles and low-voltage street lighting evoking an Eastern Bloc backwardness. Then came the neon lights of capitalism. The changes were most noticeable in the post-revolution years, but the commercialisation has continued apace. Thankfully, in the centre, the burghers have kept a check on development, except at Wenceslas Square (Václavské náměstí), which has lost some of its art nouveau glamour. Those areas remaining untouched are also protected by a UNESCO World Heritage listing and the fact that Prague's unspoilt cityscape provides an ideal cinematic backdrop.

More recently, the local design industry has been enjoying a renaissance. The annual Designblok festival, held each October, had more than 200 participants at the last count, and is testament to a burgeoning creative scene that has led to the launch of galleries such as Dvorak Sec Contemporary (see p036), where the focus is on Slovak and Czech talent. Emerging artists are nurtured at DOX (see p034), a multipurpose arts centre which is located in Holešovice, an area which is off the beaten path, but whose lively club culture and creative hotspots point to a growing urbanity. The rest of the city can seem riddled with tourist-lined cobblestoned streets and cheap Bohemian crystal, but come with us and you'll see that Prague has a modern, sophisticated side too.

ESSENTIAL INFO

FACTS, FIGURES AND USEFUL ADDRESSES

TOURIST OFFICE
Prague Information Service
Staroměstské náměstí 1
T 221 714 444
www.praguewelcome.cz

TRANSPORT
Airport transfer to city centre
www.cedaz.cz
From 7.30am to 7pm, buses depart every
30 minutes. The journey takes 30 minutes
Metro
T 296 191 817
www.dpp.cz
Trains run from 5am to midnight, and from
5am to 1am on Fridays and Saturdays
Taxis
AAA Radiotaxi
T 222 333 222
Cabs can be hailed at taxi points but it
is advisable to book one in advance
Travel Card
Unlimited 72-hour travel on buses, trams,
metro and the funicular costs CZK310

EMERGENCY SERVICES
Emergencies
T 112
24-hour pharmacy
Lékárna Palackého
Palackého 5
T 224 946 982

EMBASSIES
British Embassy
Thunovská 14
T 257 402 1111
www.ukinczechrepublic.fco.gov.uk
US Embassy
Tržiště 15
T 257 022 000
prague.usembassy.gov

POSTAL SERVICES
Post office
Jindřišská 14
T 221 132 113
Shipping
UPS
T 800 181 111
www.ups.com

BOOKS
Art-Nouveau Prague by Petr Wittlich
and Jan Malý (University of Chicago Press)
Prague: An Architectural Guide by
Radomíra Sedláková (Arsenale Editrice)
Utz by Bruce Chatwin (Vintage Classics)

WEBSITES
Architecture
www.praguearchitecture.com
Art/Design
www.ngprague.cz
Newspaper
www.praguepost.com

EVENTS
Designblok
www.designblok.cz
Prague Biennale
www.praguebiennale.org

COST OF LIVING
**Taxi from Václav Havel Airport
to the city centre**
CZK500
Cappuccino
CZK75
Packet of cigarettes
CZK75
Daily newspaper
CZK20
Bottle of champagne
CZK1,635

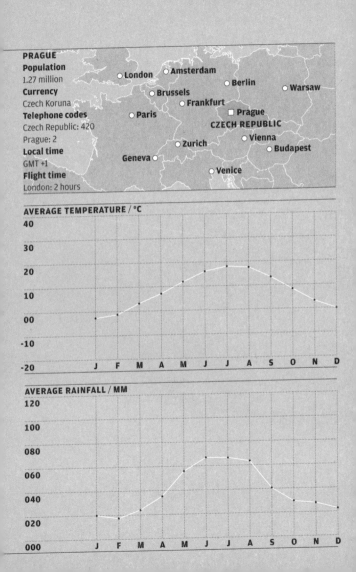

PRAGUE
Population
1.27 million
Currency
Czech Koruna
Telephone codes
Czech Republic: 420
Prague: 2
Local time
GMT +1
Flight time
London: 2 hours

○ London   ○ Amsterdam
   ● Berlin   ○ Warsaw
○ Brussels
   ○ Frankfurt
○ Paris   □ Prague
         CZECH REPUBLIC
      ○ Vienna
○ Zurich   ○ Budapest
Geneva ○
      ○ Venice

AVERAGE TEMPERATURE / °C

40

30

20

10

00

-10

-20
   J F M A M J J A S O N D

AVERAGE RAINFALL / MM

120

100

080

060

040

020

000
   J F M A M J J A S O N D

NEIGHBOURHOODS

THE AREAS YOU NEED TO KNOW AND WHY

To help you navigate the city, we've chosen the most interesting districts (see below and the map inside the back cover) and colour-coded our featured venues, according to their location; those venues that are outside these areas are not coloured.

HRADČANY

This rocky outcrop dominates the capital. It's the location of the Czech parliament and Prague Castle (see p009), whose extensive walls enclose palaces, various churches and a monastery. Visitors hustle for a place to watch the changing of the guard and to take in the mix of architectural styles. On the way down, escape the crowds by using the less-trodden routes through beautiful hillside gardens.

NOVÉ MĚSTO/VYŠEHRAD

Between the strikingly modern extension of the neo-Renaissance National Theatre (see p066) and the art nouveau slopes of Wenceslas Square, lies the consumer-oriented side of Prague. There are hordes of tourists, but you'll also see locals going about their daily business. Highlights include Frank Gehry and Vladimír Milunić's Dancing House (see p014) and the craggy formation of Vyšehrad, home to the ruin of Prague's second castle (see p009).

MALÁ STRANA

The apron of land below Prague Castle is where you'll find embassies occupying baroque palaces, and luxe hotels such as the Augustine (see p020) and the Mandarin Oriental (Nebovidská 459/1, T 233 088 888) on narrow cobblestoned streets. Small parks dot the area leading to Charles Bridge, near which you'll find the Cukrkávalimonáda café (see p048). The Petřín Tower (see p013) overlooks it all.

JOSEFOV

Discrimination against the Jews who lived here was reduced in part during the reign of the emperor Josef II, after whom the area was named; synagogues surround the old cemetery. Rudolfinum concert hall (Alšovo nábřeží, T 227 059 111) is the most formal of the area's music venues. Prague's chicest shops are on Pařížská, a street that also boasts the upmarket eaterie Cantinetta Fiorentina (see p059).

ŽIŽKOV/VINOHRADY

Separated from the city's historic centre by the ugly, north-south *magistrála* (dual carriageway), these two boroughs reflect the everyday life of Prague. Vinohrady takes its name from the vineyards that once covered this area, and its neo-Renaissance and art nouveau houses speak of previous wealth. Working-class Žižkov has a tougher feel. Visit the imposing National Memorial (see p010) and communist-era TV tower (see p068).

STARÉ MĚSTO

A mishmash of lanes surrounds Old Town Square (Staroměstske náměsti), the site of the Town Hall's famous astronomical clock. This vast open area is a great place to spot some of Prague's 100 spires, particularly those on the Disney-esque Týn Church (see p012). It's a full-on tourist trap, with pavement cafés and 'genuine' Bohemian crystal, but classier venues such as V Zátiší (see p055) are also to be found nearby.

LANDMARKS

THE SHAPE OF THE CITY SKYLINE

There is no escaping history in Prague. Here, the most noticeable and impressive landmarks occupy the prime locations. Hradčany is, without doubt, where you'll find the king of them all – Prague Castle (Hradčanské náměstí. T 224 373 368). Enter the complex through the gates guarded by Ignác Platzer's ferocious baroque statues. To the south, Vyšehrad (V Pevnosti 159/5b, T 241 410 348), the city's secondary castle, is less touristy and there's plenty to explore including an 11th-century rotunda. Between these two rocky outcrops, most of Prague lies on the plain of the Vltava River. City planners first overcame the problem of flooding by moving the street level up one floor. But the floods of 2002, the worst in centuries, were more troublesome. It took years, but new defence barriers were eventually completed.

Other key sights are often cheek by jowl and can be difficult to appreciate fully, such as the buildings around Staroměstské náměstí (Old Town Square), which range from the Romanesque and Gothic, such as Týn Church (see p012), to the rococo. However, the older parts of the city do preserve their charm by remaining free of high-rises. For the best overview, head to Malá Strana and the top of Petřín Tower (see p013). From here, you can pick out the two modernist insertions of the Tower Park (see p068) and the colossal National Memorial (overleaf) across the river.
For full addresses, see Resources.

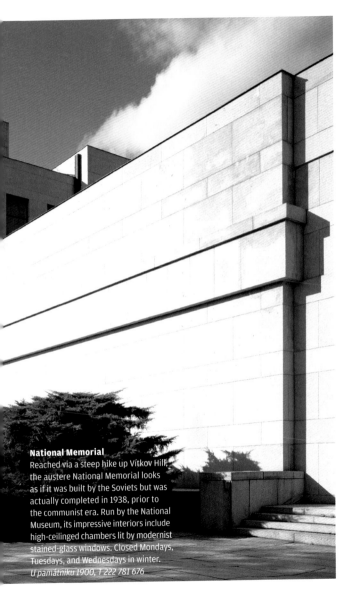

National Memorial

Reached via a steep hike up Vítkov Hill, the austere National Memorial looks as if it was built by the Soviets but was actually completed in 1938, prior to the communist era. Run by the National Museum, its impressive interiors include high-ceilinged chambers lit by modernist stained-glass windows. Closed Mondays, Tuesdays, and Wednesdays in winter. *U památníku 1900, T 222 781 676*

Týn Church

Prague is known as the city of a hundred spires, and there is no better place to start your count than here. The spiky, cartoon-like towers of the Church of Our Lady Before Týn are visible from all over the city. Brightly lit at night, they become part of the backdrop to Old Town Square; when the lights go out, they loom demonically over the narrow streets below. Although the church was completed in 1350, the towers, topped with a myriad of ornately baubled barbs, weren't finished until 1510. Note their asymmetry: the thicker, more masculine spire is located to the south, protecting the slimmer, feminine tower to the north from the sun. The church is open Tuesday to Saturday from 10am to 1pm and 3pm to 5pm, and on Sundays for morning and evening mass. *Celetná 5, T 222 318 186, www.tyn.cz*

Petřín Tower

The ideal place to survey the city skyline and Prague Castle is from the top of this observation tower in Petřín Park. If it looks suspiciously like the Eiffel Tower, that's because it's a 1:5-scale replica, built from recycled railway tracks for Prague's 1891 Jubilee Exhibition. Take the lift or the stairs to the viewing platform for a different perspective over Malá Strana and the Old Town across the Vltava. The park itself, once vineyards, is a handsome collection of lawns, orchards, waterfalls and pavilions. Look out for the onion domes that top the wooden Church of St Michael (Kinského zahrada), moved here from Ukraine in 1929, and the observatory. If you don't feel like walking, a funicular railway offers a more direct route up. *Petřínské sady, T 724 911 497, www.petrinska-rozhledna.cz*

Nationale-Nederlanden Building

Dubbed the Dancing House, this striking piece of architecture, designed by Frank Gehry in collaboration with Vladimir Milunić of Studio VM, gets additional exposure thanks to its location right next to the river. As is often the case with contemporary intrusions, the 1996 building has as many detractors as fans. Gehry's remarks that he pinched it in at the waist so that neighbours' views wouldn't be spoilt were greeted with scepticism by those who think that the building is little more than an advert for his architecture at the expense of this historic city. The good news is that a trip to make up your own mind is made all the more worthwhile by a visit to Céleste (T 221 984 160), the acclaimed French restaurant set over its top floors: a meal here comes with some outstanding views of the city thrown in.

Rašínovo nábřeží 80

HOTELS

WHERE TO STAY AND WHICH ROOMS TO BOOK

Hotels continue to open in Prague, and the resultant oversupply represents good news for visitors on two fronts. Firstly, pricing is very competitive, and secondly, savvy operators have been busy refurbishing their existing properties to keep pace. One example is the Four Seasons (Veleslavínova 1098/2a, T 221 427 000), which provides unsurpassed views across the Vltava River, and has kept up to speed with a sensitive makeover by French designer Pierre-Yves Rochon, finished in 2013. Hotel Josef (see p024) was Prague's first design hotel when it opened in 2002, and was followed by an assortment of high-tech, contemporary accommodation including The Icon (V Jámě 6, T 221 634 100), and Hotel Moods (Klimentská 28, T 222 330 100), which opened in 2010 and offers guests Mac-powered bedrooms that glow with LEDs.

Among the city's upscale properties are the elegant Augustine (see p020) and Kempinski Hybernská (see p022), whereas the Buddha-Bar Hotel (Jakubská 649/8, T 221 776 300) caters to more of a party crowd. Offerings from mainstream chains include the Charles Square Hotel (Žitná 8, T 225 999 999) – the first Sheraton in the Republic. A good independent alternative is Fusion Hotel (Panská 1308/9, T 226 222 800), which opened in 2012. Features by the building's original architect, Josef Gočár, who also designed House at the Black Madonna (see p071), have been preserved.
For full addresses and room rates, see Resources.

Dear Reader, books by Phaidon are recognized worldwide for their beauty, scholarship and elegance. We invite you to return this card with your name and e-mail address so that we can keep you informed of our new publications, special offers and events. Alternatively, visit us at **www.phaidon.com** to see our entire list of books, videos and stationery. Register on-line to be included on our regular e-newsletters.

Subjects in which I have a special interest

☐ General Non-Fiction   ☐ Art   ☐ Photography   ☐ Architecture   ☐ Design

☐ Fashion   ☐ Music   ☐ Children's   ☐ Food   ☐ Travel

	Mr/Miss/Ms	Initial	Surname
Name			
No./Street			
City			
Postcode/Zip code		Country	
E-mail			

This is not an order form. To order please contact Customer Services at the appropriate address overleaf.

Please delete address not required before mailing

PHAIDON PRESS LIMITED

Regent's Wharf

All Saints Street

London N1 9PA

UK

PHAIDON PRESS INC.

180 Varick Street

New York

NY 10014

USA

Return address for USA and Canada only

Return address for UK and countries
outside the USA and Canada only

Boscolo

Formerly known as the Carlo IV and now belonging to the Italian Boscolo group, this landmark near the old-town centre makes a striking architectural statement. The drama begins in the lobby, a former banking hall, where gilt and marble greet you at every turn. Adam D Tihany designed the restaurant and the adjacent backlit Inn Ox Lounge, which is positioned beneath a chandelier of upturned glass bottles; nearby pillars are draped in organza-like steel curtaining. Many of the guest rooms, however, veer towards the chintzy; we recommend opting for the more elegant Junior Suite (above), with its impressive ceiling. One of the hotel's best features is the decent-sized stone-lined pool under the basement arches (overleaf). *Senovážné náměstí 13, T 224 593 111, www.prague.boscolohotels.com*

Pool, Boscolo

Augustine Hotel

Fashioned around seven buildings, one of which dates back to the 13th century, this hotel takes its name from the adjacent Augustine monastery. Interiors by Olga Polizzi and London-based RDD reflect the monastic theme – as do treatments in the spa (see p089) – with a pared-down decor that incorporates local references such as cubist-inspired furniture, wrought-iron and glass. We like the Deluxe Castle

View Suite 325 (above) for its four-poster bed and spacious bathroom with heated marble flooring. The private St Thomas Brewery bar is replete with stalactites and stalagmites, while the Lichfield Café & Bar features a baroque ceiling fresco depicting four angels; in summer the bar extends out to the sheltered cloisters (opposite).
Letenská 12/33, T 266 112 233, www.theaugustine.com

Kempinski Hybernská
Planned as an apartment hotel, the Kempinski is set within a meticulously restored 17th-century property, with interiors by RPW Design. The rooms, such as 405 (pictured), are some of the most spacious in town (the average is 51 sq m), and many of them overlook the hotel's exclusive courtyard garden. *Hybernská 12, T 226 226 111, www.kempinski-prague.com*

Hotel Josef

She may be based in London, but Czech-born architect Eva Jiřičná has a soft spot for her Prague hotel project, the Josef, which she designed inside and out. The all-white lobby features her spiralling glass staircase (above), and the 109 guest rooms are divided between two blocks, the Pink and Orange Houses, which are linked by an emerald lawn where guests can enjoy breakfast in the summer. Glassed-in bathrooms in most of the accommodations help to counteract their relatively compact dimensions. Some, such as Room 801 (opposite), have a balcony and offer appealing views of Prague Castle (see p009) from the bath. Josef's central location means it is ideally placed for dining out: the impressive La Degustation Bohême Bourgeoise (see p040) and Lokál (see p054) are both in the vicinity.
Rybná 20, T 221 700 111,
www.hoteljosef.com

Hotel Praha

The heavily gated entrance to the Praha, complete with a bronzed mirrored-glass checkpoint, is a reminder of the building's origins as the hospitality centre of the Czech Communist Party. Renovated and reopened as a hotel in 1981, its sweeping balconies follow the contours of the slopes to the city's north. The somewhat austere interiors of the rooms are compensated for by their vast size, the mosaic-patterned bathrooms and the city views from the balconies – every room has one. Descend from the lobby via a flaring marble staircase to the restaurant Lavande Cuisine, which serves Czech and international fare (available on the terrace in summer), or simply wander through the numerous public areas to appreciate 1970s design at its best. *Sušická 20, T 224 341 111, www.htlpraha.cz*

987 Hotel

This 1800s apartment building opened as a hotel after a sophisticated 2006 redesign by architects GCA. Decorated in a subdued palette of taupe, burnt orange and grey, the reception area is dominated by low loungers and an arresting light installation by Kundalini. The hotel's 80 rooms feature designer pieces, such as Le Corbusier LC2 chairs, scattered throughout, and have Philippe Starck bathrooms that are fitted with bold orange glass doors. The sixth-floor Junior Suites, including Room 605 (above), are the most spacious, and some of them have terraces that overlook the city rooftops. Breakfast is served in the hotel restaurant (opposite), which also offers a light European menu from 7am to 2pm, and from 7pm to 11pm. *Senovážné náměstí 15, T 255 737 200, www.987hotels.com*

Hotel Three Storks
Formerly known as Dům U Tří Čápů,
this one-time brewery, founded by
Augustine monks in the 14th century,
was converted by architect Petr Vágner
with a view to keeping the historic fabric
of the building intact. Its 20 rooms (No
12, pictured), display a mixture of wide
oak boards, sheepskin rugs, indirect
lighting and bold splashes of colour.
Valdštejnské náměstí 8, T 257 210 779

24 HOURS
SEE THE BEST OF THE CITY IN JUST ONE DAY

Historic buildings round every corner, spires at practically every turn – sightseeing in central Prague can feel claustrophobic. But it is a wonderful city to amble around, aside from the cobblestones, perhaps. If you need a rest from walking, let a chauffeur from 3 Veteráni (Pařižská 934/2, T 603 521 700) take you for a spin in a 1932 open-top Škoda, or hop on a tram (route 22 is a good tour). The metro system is worth at least one trip, if only to experience some of the world's steepest and fastest escalators, not forgetting the platform walls, lined with shiny, lozenge-like dimpled tiles.

The city boasts several public galleries, the most impressive of which is the stern 1930s Veletržní Palace (Dukelských hrdinů 47, T 224 301 111), which houses the National Gallery's collection of modern art. In Holešovice, DOX (see p034) gets in on the 'design is art' act, and in Žižkov, Drdova Gallery (Krizkovskeho 10, T 777 216 416) represents a stable of young Czech and Slovak artists.

Out of season, without the tourists, nothing beats getting lost in the narrow streets of Staré Město. After, have lunch at Sansho (see p042) and once you've walked the cobbles of Staroměstské náměstí, visit Papelote (see p084), a store selling delicate recycled stationery. Perhaps the best way to spend a few idle afternoon hours is by the Vltava River, in particular Na Kampě, a tranquil waterfront island featuring sculptures by Czech artist David Černý. *For full addresses, see Resources.*

09.00 Café Savoy

This former department store boasts a neo-Renaissance ceiling that was hidden from view during the communist era. Now its chandeliered extravagance, overseen by the Ambiente group, is clear for all to see. Sit at a window table overlooking the leafy square outside and order a coffee and pastry, or the all-day Savoy Breakfast, which includes a juicy portion of Prague ham, Emmental cheese and a boiled egg, served with little porcelain ramekins of horseradish and homemade ginger mustard. Their silver tops are removed with an artistic flourish that will put a smile on your face. When you leave, take the route 12 tram (the stop is on Újezd) for a trip past the sites of Malá Strana and on towards Holešovice and the DOX complex (overleaf).
Vítězná 5, T 257 311 562, www.ambi.cz

11.00 DOX

Prague's DOX Centre for Contemporary Art has played a key role in kickstarting the gentrification of the gritty northern suburb of Holešovice. Founded by Leoš Válka and opened in October 2008, it is one of the few independent Czech art institutions; David Černý's controversial *Entropa* sculpture, exhibited here in 2009, is typical of the edgy works that visitors can expect. Prague-based architects Ivan Kroupa added to an existing cluster of industrial buildings to create a spacious complex, where vast white planes are linked by polished concrete staircases and ramps. Designshop on the ground floor sells glass and porcelain products curated by Qubus (see p086), or you can snap up vintage design magazines and art books at BenDOX. DOX is closed on Tuesdays. *Poupětova 1, T 295 568 123, www.dox.cz*

15.00 Dvorak Sec Contemporary
Rudolf Netik, the architect responsible for
this Josefov gallery, knows a thing or two
about display. His work at many of the
stores along Prague's upscale shopping
street, Pařížská, including Versace and
Ermenegildo Zegna, testifies to this. In
2009 he brought Olga Dvořák's and Petr
Šec's nearby art venue to life, installing
his signature cut-outs into the space,
drawing the eye from the street-level
gallery to the area below. Gallerists
and art consultants Dvořák and Šec are
particularly keen to promote talented
Slovak and Czech artists, such as the
Vsetín-born glass specialist Václav Cigler
('Hledání řádu', right). The 800 sq m,
two-storey gallery also has a terraced
area for outdoor sculptures. Dvorak
Sec is open from Monday to Friday,
and at weekends by appointment only.
Dlouhá 5, T 607 262 617
www.dvoraksec.com

22.00 Nebe Křemencova

Tucked inconspicuously into a cavernous basement in Nové Město, Nebe (meaning 'Heaven') is one of a chain of three in the city, attracting a friendly mix of youthful clubbers. The stonework of the venue's medieval ceiling is spectacular, and is illuminated by futuristic lantern-style lighting. There is plenty of space in which to appreciate your surroundings once perched alongside the gleaming orange-and-yellow backlit bar that runs the length of the side wall, or you could take up position in one of the comfortable white-upholstered booths nearby. The club's playlist tends towards pop and general mainstream sounds, but rest assured that the dancefloor will be heaving well into the early hours. Closed Sundays.
Křemencova 10, T 608 644 784, www.nebepraha.cz

URBAN LIFE
CAFÉS, RESTAURANTS, BARS AND NIGHTCLUBS

The Czech Republic is the true home of *pivo* (lager). Staropramen is still made in the capital, or you could try pilsners from Plzeň, such as Pilsner Urquell and Gambrinus, or Budweiser Budvar, not to be confused with its watery US namesake. Local hostelries tend towards the Bavarian drinking vernacular – open halls with tables and benches – and more beers will arrive without you ordering them, as there is a tacit assumption you'll continue drinking. For beer served in dimpled glass tankards, try U Zlatého Tygra (Husova 228/17, T 222 221 111). In the main, however, Prague's bar and club scene is moving in a style-oriented, cocktail-focused direction, as reflected in Hemingway Bar (Karolíny Světlé 26, T 773 974 764) and Black Angel's Bar (Staroměstské náměstí 29, T 224 213 807).

The local culinary scene is also evolving beyond the traditional standards of pork, dumplings and cabbage. Enterprising foreign restaurateurs such as Sanjiv Suri and Nils Jebens, who run the Zátiší and Kampa groups respectively, are now joined by the former Nobu London sous-chef Paul Day, who helms Sansho (see p042); and the Ambiente Restaurant Group, whose La Degustation Bohême Bourgeoise (Haštalská 18, T 222 311 234) netted a Michelin star in 2012. Other notable additions to the city's restaurant scene include CottoCrudo (T 221 426 880) at the Four Seasons (see p016), which introduced Prague to its first (and only) crudo bar.
For full addresses, see Resources.

Katr

The sounds and the scents of sizzling meat set the rhythm and pace of this restaurant, which opened in 2012 to serve organic meat and fish, from Argentinean beef to regional Czech lamb. The design is a showcase of functionality by local firm De.fakto, who divided the three rooms with white oak frames, and added blackboards that feature menus and candid reviews written by customers. In a hands-on twist, diners are encouraged to cook the meat themselves using gas hobs fitted to each veneer table, pulling down chrome ventilation hoods from the ceiling. Those not suited to DIY can request their fare cooked-to-order, or choose dishes from the à la carte menu, such as roast chicken stuffed with chestnuts and truffle oil. *Vězeňská 9, T 222 315 148, www.katrrestaurant.cz*

Sansho

British chef Paul Day is making an impact
in Prague with his South-East Asian fusion
cuisine, served in an informal dining
space. The CZK850 dinner menu includes
pork belly and watermelon salad, made
with rare-breed Prestik pig, whereas the
lunchtime à la carte service spices things
up, offering salmon sashimi with citrus
soy. Closed Sundays and Mondays.
Petrská 25, T 222 317 425, www.sansho.cz

Kavárna Pražírna

In a city where finding good coffee can be hit and miss, Pražírna is a mandatory stop. Owner Vanda Zumrová roasts beans twice weekly on site, sourcing speciality batches from small coffee farms in Cuba, Mexico, Panama and Kenya. Baristas brew with the kind of gravitas that will make a coffee aficionado sing, and snacks here include homemade cakes, panini and hops-flavoured soft drinks from the Černá

Horna brewery in South Moravia. This basement café – its shelves stacked with second-hand books – has a cosy feel; the vaulted brick ceilings, varnished timber floors and spruce beam bar were designed by Edit! Architects. Photographs by Jitka Horázná adorn the walls whenever there's no exhibition on display. Closed Sundays.
Lublaňská 50, T 720 385 622,
www.kavarnaprazirna.cz

Francouzská Restaurant

The French restaurant at Municipal House features stunning art nouveau interiors, including works by Alphonse Mucha. This is a traditional sort of place, where white-shirted waiting staff dash between the rows of tables in the grand dining hall (above). The kitchen produces European and Czech specialities and is presided over by chef Jacques Auffrays. Opt for an early supper and there will still be time to take in a performance in one of the Municipal House's concert halls. The gluttonous brunch on the first Sunday of the month is more banquet than buffet: it attracts Prague's who's who and the foie gras, game and champagne flow freely.
Náměstí Republiky 5, T 222 002 770,
www.francouzskarestaurace.cz

Cloud 9 Sky Bar & Lounge

Encased in floor-to-ceiling glass and with unobstructed views over the Vltava River, this rooftop bar in the Hilton hotel was designed by Philip Rodgers and opened in 2008. Cloud 9 is reached by walking through a theatrical, LED-lit catwalk-like hallway, a glamorous entrance that pairs well with the crowd of snappily dressed Czechs and expats. Drinks are on the expensive side, but allow yourself at least a taste of something crafted by Roman Uhlíř, one of the city's finest master bartenders. The aged signature cocktails are a good bet – the glittering skyline view calls for a Manhattan made with Maker's Mark bourbon and matured in an oak cask. Closed Sundays.
Pobřežní 1, T 224 842 999, www.cloud9.cz

Cafe-Cafe

Unlike many of Prague's coffee houses, Cafe-Cafe is not the sort of place where you'll find people with their noses buried in Kafka's *The Metamorphosis*. Its playful atmosphere instead draws the city's gay community, fashionistas and celebrity patrons. If you're near Wenceslas Square, the café is well placed for an afternoon coffee or pastry; it's famed for a sugary rota of treats including cakes like the

Black Forest gateau, and *koláč*, a classic Czech pastry imbued with fruit such as plums or cherries. The interior features art deco-style stools, a fuchsia-coloured bar, oversized mirrors and exposed brickwork and vents. During the summer, grab a table on the outside terrace facing Rytířská, which affords an excellent view of the throng passing by.

Rytířská 10, T 224 210 597, www.cafecafe.cz

Cukrkávalimonáda
Owner Tomáš Kysela designed the pared-down interior of this intimate dining venue, which serves a range of pastries, salads and cakes, as well as simple, tasty dishes like tagliatelle with fresh spinach. Daily specials usually involve some variation on trout, but are dependent on whatever happens to be available at the market on the day.
Lázeňská 7, T 257 225 396

Jazz Dock

Architect Pavel Suchý's punchy interiors in this 2009 jazz venue incorporate a candy colour-scheme offset by an acid-yellow 'futuristic-cubistic' bar front made of reflective laminate. Specialist acoustic interventions reflect the importance of music to the owner, Vladimír Lederer, who, with his partner, Karla Fišerová, was inspired to create an affordable club that would bring jazz back to the people of Prague. The single-storey structure appears to float as if moored on a narrow side-channel of the Vltava but, in fact, Jazz Dock is grounded on the riverbank, allowing for a terrace overhanging the water. The late-night music programme, which changes every three months, tends towards younger, up-and-coming artists. *Janáčkovo nábřeží 2, T 774 058 838, www.jazzdock.cz*

Grand Café Orient

For a rare chance to experience cubist architecture up close, head to the House at the Black Madonna (see p071). Czech architect Josef Gočár was responsible for the building, including the 'living interiors'. Make your way up, past the fabulous geometric balustrade on the teardrop stairwell, to the Grand Café Orient. The furniture here, also designed by Gočár, is rather sparse but beautiful.

Ask for a table on the narrow terrace to get a closer look at the architect's facade. Wherever you sit, you can enjoy the simple menu of sandwiches and salads, and our particular favourites, the pancakes, which are offered either 'salty' or sweet.
First floor, Ovocný trh 19, T 224 224 240, www.grandcafeorient.cz

M1 Lounge
Don't be put off by the wire-glass safety
doors of M1's unassuming lobby. Once
inside, pull up a bar stool and watch the
incoming parade; a slightly older, eclectic
crowd. Or reserve a booth with a table,
designed for shisha tobacco smoking. The
space is raw industrial, with a DJ station
(spinning R&B, dubstep, hip hop), a zinc-
topped bar and an intimate VIP room.
Masná 1, T 227 195 235, www.m1lounge.com

Lokál

They like their beer in Prague, and this venue brings the traditional Bohemian beer hall concept bang up to date. Local firm Ateliér PH5 reinterpreted the interior, which features long wooden benches and illuminated wall panels decorated by graffiti artists. The Pilsner Prazdroj is served from a glass bar housing stainless-steel barrels and calibrated cooling pipes, and the food is typically Czech, although it's far from staple pub fare, with fresh ingredients sourced from local suppliers and the Czech Farmer's Market. The spicy sausages, served with horseradish and mustard, are a house speciality. *Dlouhá 33, T 222 316 265, www.lokal.ambi.cz*

V Zátiši

The name of this popular restaurant translates as 'still life', but a makeover in 2011 proved that owner Sanjiv Suri is not one to rest on his laurels. Slovak interior decorator Barbara Hamplová's redesign retains elements of the flamboyant original space by Barbora Škorpilová: the venue features glass vases from Rony Plesl, Zaha Hadid bubble-design wallpaper and a Swarovski crystal chandelier. The exhaustive menu includes wine pairings selected by sommelier/manager Libor Pavlíček, and the classic regional dishes will leave a positive impression of Czech cuisine. If you're partial to dessert wine, the Sonberk Pálava, a mix of Müller-Thurgau and Gewürztraminer varietals, is delicious with a salty cheese. *Betlémské náměstí/Liliová 1, T 222 221 155, www.vzatisi.cz*

Čestr

Since opening in February 2011 as part of the successful Ambiente Restaurant Group, Čestr has proved to be one of Prague's finest purveyors of modern Bohemian cuisine. The bright, airy interior spans a large renovated section of the former Federal Assembly building, in which Czech architect Václav Červenka of Ateliér PH5 has created a striking space punctuated by a patterned glass ceiling.

Čestr (pronounced Chester) refers to *Český strakatý skot*, a newly fashionable Czech breed of cow – a hint that the menu is heavily focused on local beef. Alongside tender steaks are many other carnivorous treats such as knuckle roasted in dark beer with butter and onion. The waiters, clad smartly in brown aprons, are quick to advise on Moravian wine.

Legerova 75/57, T 222 727 851, www.ambi.cz

SaSaZu

Holešovice is now something of a clubbing hot zone, with Mecca (T 734 155 300) and Cross Club (www.crossclub.cz) also in the vicinity. In SaSaZu, the VIP mezzanine terraces that stretch the length of the 2,500-capacity venue are the best vantage point for watching the dancers surrounding the DJ stations and the 'UFO' – a globe-shaped framework that glides through the space. When you've worked up an appetite, head to the club's decent Asian-inspired restaurant (above). Studio GAD designed its suitably dark interior with distinctive spiralling lights.
Bubenské nábřeží 306, T 284 097 455, www.sasazu.com

Cantinetta Fiorentina

Boasting large, arched windows looking out on tree-lined Pařížská, this stylish complement to Josefov's ritzy boutiques is set in a historic 1906 art nouveau building on the site of the former Pravda restaurant. The interiors — which have ornate chandeliers, and Tuscan plates lining the walls — retain a grand old-Europe setting combined with a modern flair courtesy of architect Šimon Brnada of Atelier PH6. One side of the venue is a café by day, transforming into a wine bar at night, while in the white-tableclothed restaurant area (above) diners enjoy Tuscan fare — think certified Chianina beef served with black pepper sauce and green salad, pasta or seafood, all paired with a mainly Italian wine list.

Pařížská 17, T 222 326 203,
www.cantinetta.cz

La Finestra

Seen through the window, the chefs at work in the kitchen of this brick-walled restaurant will invariably be occupied with the preparation of one of the cuts of meat in which it specialises. These are imported from Italy after being aged for six weeks, although daily specials reflect an equal emphasis on seasonal produce. La Finestra is not a place for fine dining in the grandest sense, but it does offer one of the best restaurant experiences in town, utilising trestles to serve food and decanting all red wines. The eatery's bias towards meat contrasts with co-owner Riccardo Lucque's Aromi (T 222 713 222), which primarily serves fish. Both restaurants employ super-efficient staff.
Platnéřská 90/13, T 222 325 325, www.lafinestra.cz

INSIDER'S GUIDE

ZBYNEK KRULICH, DESIGNER

After graduating from Prague's Academy of Arts, Architecture and Design in 2011, Zbynek Krulich partnered with Kristýna Malovaná to establish Morphe (www.morphe.cz), a creative studio which specialises in product, furniture and interior design. If he's not in his office on Bubenska, Krulich takes his laptop to a coffee house for meetings and inspiration. He visits the experimental art gallery/café NoD (Dlouhá 33, T 073 117 4290), as well as Mistral Café (Valentinská 11/56, T 222 317 737): 'I like Mistral's interior. From a design perspective, it's one of my favourite places.'

When buying clothes, Krulich prefers the streetwear designs at The Room by Basmatee (see p080), or independent local labels like Sistersconspiracy (Vitkova 244/8, T 060 436 3989), which creates edgy menswear, and often collaborates with young artists. His womenswear suggestions include Chatty (see p087), and No (www.nofashion.eu), for its minimalist cotton tees and silk dresses. 'I'd shop there for my girlfriend,' he says. In the evening, Krulich dines on simple rustic pasta dishes at Peperoncino (Letohradská 648/34, T 233 312 438), followed by some art-house cinema and drinks at Bio Oko (Františka Křížka 460/15, T 233 382 606). If he's going clubbing, it will be at the quirky 2 Patro (Dlouhá 729/37). In his spare time, Krulich likes to run. 'Stromovka Park is great and sometimes I do bootcamps there too,' he says.

For full addresses, see Resources.

ARCHITOUR

A GUIDE TO PRAGUE'S ICONIC BUILDINGS

Stroll through central Prague and you'll view a neat history of architectural styles: Romanesque crypts under St Vitus Cathedral (Hrad III nádvoří), the Gothic spires of Týn Church (see p012), the Renaissance Belvedere Palace at Prague Castle (see p009), and many striking baroque and rococo buildings. By the early 20th century, art nouveau and Secessionist movements had taken hold, followed by cubist and other modernist influences. Fine examples are Adolf Loos' Villa Müller (see p069) and the 1932 Villa Palička (Na Babě 9), Mart Stam's input to the Werkbund's Baba housing estate.

After the communist takeover in 1948, architectural creativity suffered. The concrete-panelled swathes of suburban housing are best seen from a distance, and the faceless blocks of many state buildings and hotel towers are also to be ignored. However, this era did see the completion of laudable structures such as Hotel Praha (see p026), Nová Scéna (see p066), the Tower Park (see p068) and the Tennis Stadium (see p088). The listing of Prague's 'historic centre' as a UNESCO World Heritage Site meant that development after the Velvet Revolution didn't get out of control. It's difficult to predict which direction the city's architecture may take, but given the furore surrounding the late Jan Kaplický's green-and-purple 'blob' proposal for the National Library, Prague's residents and politicians appear reluctant to approve anything too leftfield. *For full addresses, see Resources.*

Pedestrian Tunnel

Secreted in a valley that used to be the northern moat of Prague Castle (see p009) is a pedestrian tunnel linking deer gardens either side of the Powder Bridge. This simple creation is off the beaten track and all the better for it. A bright green lawn slopes down to the narrow elliptic tunnel created by architect Josef Pleskot of AP Atelier in 2002. The internal walls are lined with vertically placed bricks that create a woven pattern, accentuated by the lights recessed in the concrete floor. Halfway along is a niche where the remains of the preserved foundations of the original Renaissance bridge are displayed. Move up the moat's slope to the plateau, where you'll find Eva Jiřičná's first Prague building, the 1998 Orangery in the Royal Gardens of the castle.
Under U Prašného mostu

Nová Scéna

Across the plaza from the National Theatre (T 224 901 448) – built in 1883 in a neo-Renaissance style – stands Karel Prager's dramatic 1983 Nová Scéna extension (pictured), home to a square auditorium. Covered with more than 4,000 blown-glass blocks, it's best viewed at sunset when the facade glows.
Národní 4, T 224 931 482,
www.novascena.cz

Tower Park

Formerly called the Žižkov TV Tower, this spiky edifice typifies the often outlandish creations of the communist era. Three silver towers support the aerial section of the rocket-like construction. Attempts have been made to liven up its greyness, from David Černý's black *Babies* crawling up the structure, to the red under-lighting of the platforms. In 2012, Atelier SAD transformed the interiors, refurbishing the bistro and bar with modernist flair, and adding a luxury hotel suite. From the top-floor enclosed lookout deck, visitors enjoy a 360-degree view of Prague while suspended in Eero Aarnio 'Bubble Chairs'. On a clear day, the National Memorial (see p010) and the statue of the medieval general Jan Žižka almost seem touchable. *Mahlerovy sady 1, T 724 251 286, www.towerpark.cz*

Villa Müller

The culmination of Adolf Loos' Raumplan conceptualisation of residential spaces, Villa Müller was completed in 1930 and restored 70 years later. It follows a spiral plan of rooms set around a staircase. Cubist elements can be seen throughout: in the plum-and-velvet-upholstered sofa placed between two marble blocks; the radiator cover in the Japanese-inspired summer dining room; and the cubic planters on the roof terrace. From the green-grey Cipollino de Saillon marble used to clad the walls and pillars of the main hall, to the mahogany of the dining-room table and its coffered ceiling, the high-quality materials shine through thanks to Loos' laconic style. He rated the villa as his best work.
Nad hradním vodojemen 14, T 224 312 012, www.mullerovavila.cz

Emauzy Church

An American air raid in February 1945 provided the opportunity for a radical rethink of the towers for the Gothic Church of the Blessed Virgin Mary. The city of a hundred spires got two more when, after a competition, František María Černý's proposal for two interlinking wing towers was chosen. They may seem a little incongruous atop the historic institution, but the concrete structures have an admirable lightness of touch. Their elegance is best viewed from the church grounds or from the lawns of Palackého náměstí, towards the Vltava River. From there you will have the chance to see the light pass between the intersecting elements, which are meant to evoke both the single Gothic and twin baroque gables. *Vyšehradská 49, T 224 917 662, www.emauzy.cz*

House at the Black Madonna

The cubist style was utilised in several buildings during the reconstruction of the Jewish quarter, Josefov, and its surrounds. In the years preceding WWI, the movement became popular among the avant-garde in Bohemia and was commonly used in government buildings. The House at the Black Madonna, designed by Josef Gočár and built between 1911 and 1912, is one of the best examples of the style. It houses the Grand Café Orient (see p051), and on the ground floor is the Kubista Gallery (see p073). For another classic example of cubism, see the telamones on the facade of the building at Elišky Krásnohorské 7. The pink palette is in amusing contrast to their muscular torsos.
Ovocný trh 19

SHOPPING

THE BEST RETAIL THERAPY AND WHAT TO BUY

There's more to shopping in Prague than the stores on Pařížská (the city's equivalent of London's Bond Street or Rue du Faubourg Saint-Honoré in Paris), which include Rolex, Louis Vuitton and the chic designer emporium Simple Concept Store (see p076). It's on the surrounding streets of Dlouhá, Dušní and V Kolkvoně that the real heart of Czech creativity beats, so much so that eight brands based here have formed an alliance, the Czech Fashion Centre (www.czechfashion.cz), to promote their merchandise. The small production runs cultivated by its members, including menswear label Jozef Sloboda (Rytířská 11, T 224 248 971) and womenswear designers Hana Havelková (Dušní 10, T 222 326 754) and Klára Nademlýnská (Dlouhá 3, T 224 818 769), make for unique buys.

If you're interested in cubist design, Staré Město is home to two of its best purveyors: Kubista Gallery (opposite) and Modernista (Celetná 12, T 224 241 300), which sells reproduction furniture and objets d'art, as well as a selection of contemporary products, such as the fine glassware by Czech design studio Olgoj Chorchoj (www.olgojchorchoj.cz). Committed design fans should venture further out to Holešovice, location of Křehký (see p074), to pick up porcelain pieces by young Czech artists such as Maxim Velčovský. For more modern glassware, anything crafted by Tomáš Kysela, the owner of Material (Tyn 1, T 608 664 766), is sure to impress. *For full addresses, see Resources.*

Kubista Gallery

Enter through the columnar portals of the House at the Black Madonna (see p071) and turn left for the Kubista Gallery. Although service can, at times, be brusque, the shop has an exhibition-like air, with replica and restored 1920s and 1930s items on display. Cubist techniques were applied to a variety of three-dimensional wares, from lighting to pieces such as Pavlína Lubomírská's ceramic box (replica, above), CZK2,900, and have been adopted for modern jewellery design too. Kubista also stocks some reproduction furniture in limited, numbered series and will ship anywhere in the world. Its sister store, Futurista Universum (T 725 128 660), a short walk away, sells contemporary Czech design. Kubista is closed on Mondays. *Ovocný trh 19, T 224 236 378, www.kubista.cz*

Křehký
Prague-based design studio Olgoj Chorchoj transformed this former ham factory into a 2010 addition to Holešovice's burgeoning arts precinct. Gallery owners Jana Zielinski and Jiří Macek home in on original Czech designers, especially those working with glass and porcelain, such as Moravian creative Daniel Pirsc. Open Wednesday and Thursday (10am-8pm), or by appointment. *Osadni 35, T 267 990 545, www.krehky.cz*

Simple Concept Store

Modelled on the original Parisian concept boutique, Colette, Simple Concept Store follows the same principle, stocking a wide range of thoughtfully curated designer products. Czech contributions are few and far between at this fashion emporium; instead it's a glossy white temple to top French fashion houses such as Céline, Lanvin and Yves Saint Laurent. Collections are displayed artfully around the space, which features a champagne bar. Upstairs is devoted to an exclusive range of Christian Louboutin shoes, along with luxe accessories, cosmetics and fragrances by the likes of Six Scents and Creed. A select range of home products includes items by Diptyque, and there are also paintings by Czech artists for sale. *Pařížská 20, T 221 771 677, www.simpleconcept.cz*

Timoure et Group

The long-standing collaboration between Alexandra Pavalová and Ivana Šafránková has delivered an eminently practical line of womenswear. Knits and suits, shirts and skirts are arranged on stainless-steel display tables or yellow neon shelves, set off by the boutique's black epoxy floors. Architect Daniela Polubědovová's minimalist store reflects the concept behind the clothes on display. These generally greyscale pieces, with the odd splash of pastel or coloured, shiny beading, are inspired by what the two stylish women would wear themselves. It's a little more casual than several of the neighbouring boutiques and everything here is Czech-made. Timoure et Group is a member of the Czech Fashion Centre (see p072).
V Kolkovně 6, T 222 327 358,
www.timoure.com

Botas Concept Store

Like many a savvy shoe brand, Botas, which has been in the business of sports footwear for more than four decades, has a retro diffusion line, Botas 66. Its iconic 'Classic' trainers were resurrected by local design students Jakub Korouš and Jan Kloss, who proposed the project as part of their coursework at Prague's Academy of Arts, Architecture and Design. Botas snapped up their designs and the shoes are displayed in the Botas Concept Store, which includes a gallery space (above). Designed by A1 Architects, it's shaped like a number six, with bright yellow shoeboxes set into black display units (opposite). Choose from 10 classic styles, from neutral blacks to the aptly named 'Rainbow Maker', €70, a vivid kaleidoscope of colour. *Konviktská 1005/30, T 224 281 148, www.botas66.cz*

The Room by Basmatee
When Jan Lichy moved his independent design store into larger premises in 2012, he transformed it into an urban concept boutique catering to men seeking hard-to-find street-savvy clothes, shoes and accessories. Architects Skvadra refitted the space, in which floor-to-ceiling black shelves display cult shoes, and clothing hangs from the ceiling on shipping rope.
Školská 7, T 222 967 770

Konsepti

Spiral staircases – green for up and red for down – link the gallery-like spaces of Konsepti, distributor of the great and the good of local and international furniture design. Located in Holešovice, not very far from contemporary art gallery DOX (see p034), the showroom is based in a former metal factory dating to 1911, earning the store its well-deserved moniker: 'The Design Factory'. Konsepti provides interior decorating services to private homes as well as local boutiques, restaurants and hotels, including Hotel Three Storks (see p030). On sale here are items from eminent design names like Established & Sons, Driade and Philippe Starck, whose aluminium 'Abbracciaio' candle holders were designed in conjunction with Kartell. *Komunardů 32, T 266 199 452, www.konsepti.com*

Leica Gallery

Behind the sgraffito facade of the Leica Gallery is an exhibition space illuminated by the large, arched windows that line the slope of Školská, to the south-west of Wenceslas Square. A not-for-profit organisation, the gallery presents work by contemporary Czech and Slovak photographers such as Lukáš Dvořák and returned émigré Robert Vano, together with international names. Leica has an art-school feel, with a bookish café that is also used for regular seminars and workshops. The small shop sells exhibition-related merchandise and photography publications. You can view more photo exhibitions at the Galerie Fotografie Louvre (T 224 930 949) on nearby Národní. The Leica Gallery is open Monday to Friday, 8am to 9pm; weekends, 2pm to 8pm.
Školská 28, T 222 211 567, www.lgp.cz

Papelote
Quirky and colourful, Papelote's pencil cases, notebooks and recycled paper brighten up any desk. Its tiny store and workshop was designed by A1 Architects, who stripped back the walls to expose layers of plaster, and also covered the vaulted ceilings in wrapping paper. Sold alongside the brand's stationery range are Czech-made Koh-I-Noor pencils.
Vojtěšská 9, T 774 219 113

Qubus x Denim Heads

The Qubus design studio was founded by Maxim Velčovský and Jakub Berdych in 2002. The pair's products straddle glassware, ceramics and lighting, and often have a surreal edge. Take Berdych's 'Raw' lamp, for instance, an ornate black chandelier suspended from a utilitarian stand, which sits alongside items by other Czech designers including Antonín Tomášek, Milan Pekař and Hana Vítková.

In addition to design pieces, Qubus also stocks a selection of international denim, a far-reaching range launched in 2011 under the name Denim Heads. Expect to find jeans for men from Ijin Material, Denim Demon and Japan Blue, as well as T-shirts, shoes and leather accessories.
Rámová 3, T 222 313 151, www.qubus.cz

Chatty

Czech fashion designers Radka Sirková and Anna Tušková's womenswear label, Chatty, has gained a tribe of followers and high-profile clients since its inception in 2005. Garments are progressive, sharply tailored and structural, using silk, leather and denim materials. The new showroom, which opened in 2012, functions as both a workspace and a boutique. The work of architect Jiří Zhoř of Studio Muon, who also designed Mistral Café (see p062), the pared back, industrial aesthetic mirrors the sartorial concept of muted tones and texture, using steel, oak beams and raw concrete panels. As well as Chatty's own ready-to-wear clothing, the store sells leather clutches by Czech label Milimu, shoes by Slovak Zuzana Serbák and watches by Swedish brand Cheapo. *Haštalská 21, www.chatty.cz*

SPORTS AND SPAS
WORK OUT, CHILL OUT OR JUST WATCH

It would be fair to say that the historic centre of Prague is not a sporting hub – narrow cobbled streets and sloping gardens hardly inspire a run. However, just to the north of the city, either side of a busy thoroughfare, are Letenské and Stromovka parks, pleasant places to stretch your legs among the in-line skaters and frisbee throwers. Here you'll also find a couple of stadiums: the Generali Arena (Milady Horákové 1066/98, T 296 111 400), home of the Republic's top football team, Sparta Prague; and Tipsport Arena (Za elektrárnou 419/1, T 266 727 443), where ice hockey, the nation's favourite sport after football, is played. In summer, the pool complex at Podolí (see p094) provides respite from the heat. Or try a clay-court session in the shadows of the Český Lawn-Tennis Klub (Ostrov Štvanice 38, T 222 316 317). The Vltava is used for more than the odd tourist pedalo excursion to the edge of the weir; scullers take off from the Smíchov side, whereas further downstream is a world-class whitewater kayaking site (see p090).

Spa culture, on the other hand, has been slow to take off in the city. As the spa town of Karlovy Vary (see p102) is only a few hours away, this is perhaps no surprise. For the best in urban pampering, the city's top hotels are leading the way. Visit the Augustine Spa (opposite) or The Spa at Mandarin Oriental (Nebovidská 459/1, T 233 088 655) for soothing treatments in stylish surrounds. _For full addresses, see Resources._

Augustine Spa

A truly secluded environment, the spa at the Augustine Hotel (see p020) is reached via a labyrinth of passages, and the retreat has the additional bragging rights of being the only spa in the world to be located adjacent to a fully functioning monastery. Classic deep-tissue, Swedish massage and hammam treatments, using Kerstin Florian and Ila products, are augmented by the signature St Thomas Beer body treatment.

This involves finely ground hops being used as an exfoliant before the hotel's own beer (available on tap at the in-house Lichfield Café & Bar) is poured on to the body to nourish the skin. Hotel guests can use the sauna, steam room, Technogym area and relaxation room for free, whereas visitors can purchase spa day passes for CZK850. *Letenská 12/33, T 266 112 273, www.theaugustine.com*

White Water Centre

Downstream and to the north of the city,
the Vltava is a playground for paddlers.
There is plenty of flat, smooth water to
get your hand in, so to speak, before
tackling the surging torrent of the 410m-
long whitewater course that has hosted
the World Canoe Kayak Racing Slalom
Championships. All equipment (boats,
paddles, spray decks, helmets and
buoyancy aids) is available for hire at
the White Water Centre's boathouse.
These rapids are not for the faint-hearted
and the use of the hired equipment is
restricted, but tuition can be arranged
and courses are also run; opening hours
are seasonal, so check before visiting.
Alternatively, watch the experts in action
as you drink a cold beer at a prime table
in Restaurace Loděnice (T 283 850 477),
which is open from March to September.
Vodácká 789/8, T 283 850 477,
troja.kanoe.cz

AVIM Praha

It's no surprise that this tightly controlled range exists in Prague, given that the gun laws in the Czech Republic are among the most relaxed in Europe and target shooting is popular. AVIM is open to those with a Czech gun licence; those without must show ID and practise under the close supervision of an instructor. Stick to the range — the café has a grungy feel.
Sokolovská 23, T 222 329 328, www.avim.cz

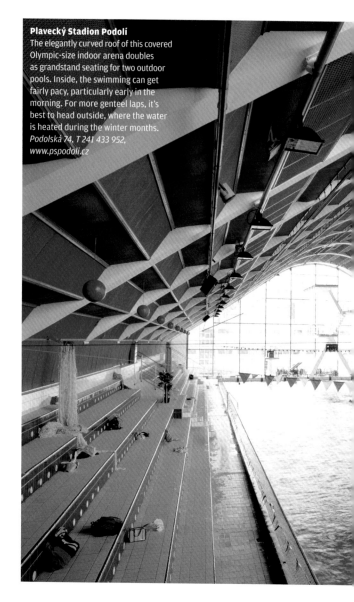

Plavecký Stadion Podolí
The elegantly curved roof of this covered Olympic-size indoor arena doubles as grandstand seating for two outdoor pools. Inside, the swimming can get fairly pacy, particularly early in the morning. For more genteel laps, it's best to head outside, where the water is heated during the winter months.
Podolská 74, T 241 433 952,
www.pspodoli.cz

ESCAPES

WHERE TO GO IF YOU WANT TO LEAVE TOWN

Prague's ever increasing popularity has unfortunately led to a city centre choked with tourists, to say nothing of the oppressive heat in summer. Instant escape is provided by the water bowsers that patrol Wenceslas Square spraying a fine mist, ostensibly to damp down the street dust. More breathing space can be found a few kilometres north of the city on the Vltava's banks. Trója Château (U Trojského zámku 1) is a bold pink baroque villa fronted by a handsome garden. The interior decor is all murals and marquetry, providing the backdrop for a collection of Czech art. While in the area, check out the kayakers on the white-water course (see p090).

Once you've made it past the frankly dull suburbs of the city, you soon reach the rolling green landscape of Bohemia. Between the woods, fields of hops line the hills – this is beer country, after all – and Plzeň (opposite) is just over an hour's drive south-west of Prague. En route, stop at Beroun to visit the arresting Karlštejn Castle (see p098). Further south, the quaint, delightfully cobbled Český Krumlov charms even the most po-faced traveller with its medieval atmosphere. The mineral spa town of Karlovy Vary (see p102) to the west, has the cachet and the crowds, while south of here, Mariánské Lázně (otherwise known as Marienbad) is an elegant alternative. Berlin and Vienna are less than five hours away by train – if you really want to escape.

For full addresses, see Resources.

Plzeň

The home of pilsner beer, Plzeň is an easy 90km drive from the capital. If you're expecting a picturesque Bohemian town, be patient as you pass the enormous Škoda works on its outskirts. Once inside the old city walls, your focus should be on the fine Gothic buildings surrounding the central square, such as the early 16th-century St Bartholomew's Cathedral (T 377 236 753); its 103m-high spire is the tallest in the country. More famous, perhaps, are Gambrinus and Pilsner Urquell, which are brewed here. Both are now owned by the South African beer giant SABMiller, which still runs the Plzeňský Prazdroj brewery (above; T 377 061 111). Tours take place daily between 11am and 4.15pm, and finish with pilsner tastings in the original cellars. In 2015, the city will share the title of European Capital of Culture with Mons.

Karlštejn Castle
This fairy-tale castle was completed in 1348 as a retreat for Charles IV. Many Gothic and Renaissance adjustments have given a dramatic look to the fortress, which rises and falls over several levels. Access to the castle, and its significant collection of Gothic art panels and murals, is by tour only.
Beroun, Karlštejn, T 311 681 617, www.hradkarlstejn.cz

Kutná Hora

A mining town might not be at the top of your list of city escapes, but Kutná Hora's Gothic splendour was bankrolled by its silver mines. The importance of the town, which is an 80-minute drive east of Prague, can be seen in the splendid St Barbara's Cathedral (opposite and above; T 327 512 115). Its roof is draped, tent-like, from three massive spires high above a forest of flying buttresses. Detailing throughout Kutná Hora, including on František Baugut's 1715 *Morový sloup* (Plague Column), features typical mining imagery. The plague led to the creation of the rather macabre Sedlec Ossuary (T 326 551 049), a chapel where the transience of life is 'celebrated' through skeletal decorations from approximately 30,000 plague victims, plus some 10,000 others. *www.kutnahora.cz*

Karlovy Vary

Home to the country's oldest golf course, and a film festival, Karlovy Vary is famous for hot springs and buildings dating from the late 1800s, when taking to the waters was de rigueur. Hotel Imperial (T 353 203 113) and Grand Hotel Pupp (T 353 109 111) evoke an impression of belle époque, and although the concrete exterior of the Hotel Thermal (T 359 002 201) is an eyesore, its outdoor pool (pictured) sweetens the deal.

NOTES

SKETCHES AND MEMOS

RESOURCES

CITY GUIDE DIRECTORY

A

Aromi 060
Mánesova 1442/78
T 222 713 222
www.aromi.cz

Augustine Spa 089
Augustine Hotel
Letenská 12/33
T 266 112 273
www.theaugustine.com

AVIM Praha 092
Sokolovská 23
T 222 329 328
www.avim.cz

B

Bio Oko 062
Františka Křížka 460/15
T 233 382 606
www.biooko.net

Black Angel's Bar 040
Staroměstské náměstí 29
T 224 213 807
www.blackangelsbar.cz

Botas Concept Store 078
Konviktská 1005/30
T 224 281 148
www.botas66.cz

C

Cafe-Cafe 047
Rytířská 10
T 224 210 597
www.cafecafe.cz

Café Savoy 033
Vítězná 5
T 257 311 562
www.ambi.cz

Cantinetta Fiorentina 059
Pařížská 17
T 222 326 203
www.cantinetta.cz

Céleste 014
Nationale-Nederlanden Building
Rašínovo nábřeží 80
T 221 984 160
www.celesterestaurant.cz

Český Lawn-Tennis Klub 088
Ostrov Štvanice 38
T 222 316 317
www.cltk.cz

Čestr 056
Legerova 75/57
T 222 727 851
www.ambi.cz

Chatty 087
Haštalská 21
www.chatty.cz

Church of St Michael 013
Kinského zahrada

Cloud 9 Sky Bar & Lounge 046
Hilton Hotel
Pobřežní 1
T 224 842 999
www.cloud9.cz

CottoCrudo 040
Four Seasons
Veleslavínova 1098/2a
T 221 426 880
www.cottocrudo.cz

Cross Club 058
Plynární 23
www.crossclub.cz

HOTELS
ADDRESSES AND ROOM RATES

Augustine Hotel 020
Room rates:
double, from €210;
Deluxe Castle View Suite 325, €1,300
Letenská 12/33
T 266 112 233
www.theaugustine.com

Boscolo 017
Room rates:
double, from €140;
Junior Suite, from €275
Senovážné náměstí 13
T 224 593 111
www.prague.boscolohotels.com

Buddha-Bar Hotel 016
Room rates:
double, from €280
Jakubská 649/8
T 221 776 300
www.buddha-bar-hotel.cz

Charles Square Hotel 016
Room rates:
double, from €150
Žitná 8
T 225 999 999
www.sheratonprague.com

Four Seasons 016
Room rates:
double, from €315
Veleslavínova 1098/2a
T 221 427 000
www.fourseasons.com/prague

Fusion Hotel 016
Room rates:
double, from €80
Panská 1308/9
T 226 222 800
www.fusionhotels.com

Grand Hotel Pupp 102
Room rates:
double, from €160
Mírové náměstí 2
Karlovy Vary
T 353 109 111
www.pupp.cz

The Icon 016
Room rates:
double, from €80
V Jámě 6
T 221 634 100
www.iconhotel.eu

Hotel Imperial 102
Room rates:
double, from €150
Libušina 18
Karlovy Vary
T 353 203 113
www.spa-hotel-imperial.cz

Hotel Josef 024
Room rates:
double, from €115;
Room 801, €250
Rybná 20
T 221 700 111
www.hoteljosef.com

Kempinski Hybernská 022
Room rates:
double, from €230;
Room 405, €435
Hybernská 12
T 226 226 111
www.kempinski-prague.com

Hotel Moods 016
  Room rates:
  double, from €100
  Klimentská 28
  T 222 330 100
  www.hotelmoods.com
987 Hotel 028
  Room rates:
  double, from €90;
  Junior Suite 605, from €150
  Senovážné náměstí 15
  T 255 737 200
  www.987hotels.com
Hotel Praha 026
  Room rates:
  double, from €75
  Sušická 20
  T 224 341 111
  www.htlpraha.cz
Hotel Three Storks 030
  Room rates:
  double, from €140;
  Room 12, from €145
  Valdštejnské náměstí 8
  T 257 210 779
  www.utricapu.cz

WALLPAPER* CITY GUIDES

Executive Editor
Rachael Moloney

Editor
Ella Marshall
Authors
Guy Dittrich
Michelle Wranik

Art Director
Loran Stosskopf
Art Editor
Eriko Shimazaki
Designer
Mayumi Hashimoto
Map Illustrator
Russell Bell

Photography Editor
Elisa Merlo
Assistant Photography Editor
Nabil Butt

Chief Sub-Editor
Nick Mee

Editorial Assistant
Emma Harrison

Intern
Romy van den Broeke

**Wallpaper* Group
Editor-in-Chief**
Tony Chambers
Publishing Director
Gord Ray
Managing Editor
Oliver Adamson

Wallpaper* ® is a
registered trademark
of IPC Media Limited

First published 2007
Revised and updated
2012 and 2013

All prices are correct at
the time of going to press,
but are subject to change.

Printed in China

PHAIDON

Phaidon Press Limited
Regent's Wharf
All Saints Street
London N1 9PA

Phaidon Press Inc
180 Varick Street
New York, NY 10014

Phaidon® is a registered
trademark of Phaidon
Press Limited

www.phaidon.com

A CIP Catalogue record for
this book is available from
the British Library.

ISBN 978 0 7148 6610 9

PHOTOGRAPHERS

Profimedia International sro/Alamy
Karlštejn Castle, pp098-099
St Barbara's Cathedral, p101

Sarah Blee
Augustine Hotel, p021
Kempinski Hybernská, pp022-023
Hotel Josef, p024
DOX, p034, p035
Jazz Dock, p050
Lokál, p054
SaSaZu, p058
La Finestra, pp060-061
Villa Müller, p069
Konsepti, p082
Augustine Spa, p089

Czech Tourism
Hotel Thermal, pp102-103

Markus Hilbich
St Barbara's Cathedral, p100

Ales Jungmann
Prague city view, inside front cover
Boscolo, p017, pp018-019
Hotel Josef, p025
987 Hotel, p028, p029
Dvorak Sec Contemporary, pp036-037
Nebe Křemencova, p038, p039
Katr, p041
Sansho, pp042-043
Kavárna Praržírna, p044
Cloud 9 Sky Bar & Lounge, p046
Cafe-Cafe, p047
Cukrkávalimonáda, pp048-049
M1 Lounge, pp052-053
V Zátiši, p055
Čestr, pp056-057
Cantinetta Fiorentina, p059
Zbynek Krulich, p063
Křehký, pp074-075
Simple Concept Store, p076
Timoure et Group, p077
Botas Concept Store, p078, p079
The Room by Basmatee, pp080-081
Leica Gallery, p083
Papelote, pp084-085
Qubus x Denim Heads, p086
Chatty, p087

Noshe
National Memorial, pp010-011
Týn Church, p012
Petřín Tower, p013
Nationale-Nederlanden Building, pp014-015
Hotel Three Storks, pp030-031
Grand Café Orient, p051
Pedestrian Tunnel, p065
Nová Scéna, pp066-067
Tower Park, p068
Emauzy Church, p070
House at the Black Madonna, p071
White Water Centre, pp090-091
AVIM Praha, pp092-093
Plavecký Stadion Podolí, pp094-095

PRAGUE
A COLOUR-CODED GUIDE TO THE HOT 'HOODS

HRADČANY
Crowds flock to the rambling citadel; the charming hillside gardens are more tranquil

NOVÉ MĚSTO/VYŠEHRAD
The commercial hub buzzes with tourists and locals alike. A ruined castle lies to the south

MALÁ STRANA
Boasting cobbled streets and baroque palaces, this is period-drama Prague at its finest

JOSEFOV
Once the city's Jewish ghetto, this quarter has been colonised by high-fashion labels

ŽIŽKOV/VINOHRADY
Communist-era grit and bourgeois sophistication coexist in these residential areas

STARÉ MĚSTO
This tourist honeypot is worth a visit for Týn Church and the unique cubist architecture

For a full description of each neighbourhood, see the Introduction.
Featured venues are colour-coded, according to the district in which they are located.